BFF Cookbook

more than **30** yummy

BFF Cookbook
recipes for friendship fun!

Susan E. DerKazarian

SCHOLASTIC INC.

New York Toronto London Auckland Sydney
Mexico City New Delhi Hong Kong

No part of this publication may be reproduced in whole or in part, or stored in a retrieval system, or transmitted in any form or by any means, electronic, mechanical, photocopying, recording, or otherwise, without written permission of the publisher. For information regarding permission, write to Scholastic Inc., Attention: Permissions Department, 555 Broadway, New York, NY 10012.

ISBN 0-439-20348-1

Designed by Lee Kaplan

Copyright © 2000 by Scholastic Inc.
All rights reserved. Published by Scholastic Inc.
SCHOLASTIC and associated logos are trademarks and/or registered trademarks of Scholastic Inc.

12 11 10 9 8 7 6 5 4 3 2 1   0 1 2 3 4 5/0

Printed in the U.S.A.
First Scholastic printing, August 2000

To my mother, Isabelle, a great cook who taught me that cooking can be fun!

Contents

Fun, Friends, and Cooking! 1

Cooking Basics 2

Rise 'n' Shine! 3

After-school Snacks 13

Quick Lunch and Dinner Dishes 23

Best Beverages, Super Shakes! 38

The Sweet Stuff 46

Party Planning 55

Holiday Food Ideas 71

Keep on Cookin'! 83

Recipes of My Own 86

Fun, Friends, and Cooking!

Cooking is fun. And cooking with friends is even more fun.

The yummy recipes in this book are great to make together with a friend — or a bunch of friends. So the next time you and your buds are wondering what to do, why not make yourselves a treat? You'll also find some great party-food ideas that are as fun to make as they are to eat!

Every recipe in this book is geared to kids your age. They are easy to make, and you won't need an adult helping you every step of the way. Some of the recipes might require an adult's help on a step or two, but you'll be able to do most of the preparations yourself! When you see this symbol 🧑‍🍳 in a recipe, it means you'll need an adult's help with that recipe.

Enjoy!

Cooking Basics

Here are some basic tips to help you be a good cook:

1. Read the recipe *carefully* before you begin. You'll want to be sure you have all the ingredients and utensils you'll need.

2. Wash your hands.

3. Put on an apron to protect your clothes.

4. Take out all the ingredients and utensils you will need to do the whole recipe and spread them out where you are going to work.

5. Be sure to have a grown-up to help you when you see the 👨‍🍳 symbol in a recipe. Your grown-up will handle most of the stove and oven steps and using a knife.

6. Clean up after yourself when you are done cooking — wipe up spills and put everything away.

And last but not least:

7. Don't worry if you make a cooking mistake. That's how cooks learn!

Rise 'n' Shine!

Nutrition experts (the people who know what foods are good for you) say that breakfast is the most important meal of the day. If you fuel up in the morning you'll have enough energy to get your day off to a great start! Here are four delicious breakfast recipes that will have you jumping out of bed in the morning!

Fruit Funnies (or Breakfast on a Stick)

Here's a fun way to eat fruit. It's a perfect way to start the day! This recipe serves you and three friends.

Ingredients You Will Need:

1 orange

1 banana

1 apple

1 pear

Three 8-ounce containers yogurt in different flavors

Utensils You Will Need:

Butter knife

Paring knife

4 wooden skewers

3 small bowls

What You Do:

1. Peel the orange and separate the slices.

2. Peel the banana. Using the butter knife, cut the banana into chunks about one inch thick.

3. 🧑‍🍳 Wash the apple and pear. Then cut them into slices using the paring knife.

4. You and your friends each take a wooden skewer. Put about six pieces of fruit on each skewer. Alternate the different types of fruit.

5. Open the containers of yogurt. Put each flavor into its own bowl.

Now you and your pals can dip your pieces of skewered fruit into the yogurt. Be creative with fruit-yogurt combinations. For example, bananas taste great dipped in strawberry yogurt.

Breakfast Banana Split

Here is a great way to jazz up plain cereal and turn it into a special breakfast concoction. This tasty recipe serves you and a friend.

Ingredients You Will Need:

1 banana

One 8-ounce container vanilla yogurt

1 cup cereal (rice cereal and granola are good choices, but you can use whatever is your and your friend's favorite type of cereal)

1 cup fresh, washed blueberries

Utensils You Will Need:

2 cereal bowls

Butter knife

2 spoons

What You Do:

1. Peel the banana. Using the butter knife, cut it in half lengthwise. Put one half in one bowl, and half into the other.

2. Open the container of yogurt and spoon half of it into one bowl, and half into the other bowl.

3. Sprinkle ½ cup of cereal onto the yogurt in one bowl, and half onto the yogurt in the other bowl.

4. Sprinkle ½ cup of blueberries into one bowl, and half into the other.

Now dig in for a creamy, crunchy, fruity breakfast! You don't have to follow this recipe exactly, you know. For example, if you like strawberry-flavored yogurt better than vanilla, no problem! If you want to use raspberries instead of blueberries, go right ahead. You can make this recipe whatever way YOU like!

Blue Letter Pancakes

Here's another delicious (and sweet!) way to start the day. These pancakes are especially fun to make with friends because each person gets to "sign" her own pancakes — with blueberries! The recipe makes about 12 medium-size pancakes, enough for four to six friends. (If you want, you can start with ready-made pancake batter and skip right to step 6.)

Ingredients You Will Need:

1½ cups flour
½ teaspoon salt
3 tablespoons sugar
1¾ teaspoon baking powder
2 eggs
About half a stick of butter
1¼ cups milk
1 cup fresh, washed blueberries
Maple syrup

Utensils You Will Need:

Measuring cups and spoons
Medium-size bowl
2 small bowls
Fork
Wire whisk
Wooden spoon
Skillet
Pancake flipper or spatula
Range top of oven
4 to 6 plates

What You Do:

1. In the medium-size bowl, add the flour, salt, sugar, and baking powder. Use a fork to mix the ingredients together well.

2. Gently tap an egg against the edge of one of the small bowls so it cracks but doesn't mash open. Then open the two halves of the eggshell over the bowl and let the raw egg drop into the bowl. Repeat with the second egg.

3. 👨‍🍳 Melt two tablespoons of butter. You can do this on the stove top in the skillet, or you can microwave the butter on medium-high for about 10 seconds.

4. Add the melted butter and the milk to the eggs. Using the wire whisk, whip the ingredients together until there aren't any more big chunks of yellow egg yolk.

5. Pour the egg-butter-milk mixture into the flour-salt-sugar-baking-powder mixture and stir together with the wooden spoon. Stir just until the ingredients are mixed together, and don't worry if there are lumps! If you stir too much the pancakes might not end up being nice and fluffy.

6. 👨‍🍳 Turn on the oven burner to medium. Add a small chunk of butter to the skillet and swirl the melted butter around so it covers the bottom of the skillet.

7. Dip the ¼ or ½ measuring cup into the pancake batter and fill it up as much as you can. Slowly and carefully pour a little of the batter onto the skillet until the batter makes a circle that's about four inches across at the widest point. Depending on how big your skillet is, you may be able to fit up to three pancakes on it at once.

8. Let the pancakes cook for about a minute and then carefully drop blueberries onto a pancake so you spell out the first letter of your first name. Do this with all the pancakes that are going to be yours. Do the same for your friends' pancakes.

9. When you see air bubbles on the top of the pancake, carefully slide the pancake flipper or spatula under the pancake and flip it over to cook the other side. Cook the other side of the pancake for about a minute, then flip it over again and check out the letter you created with blueberries — your "signature"!

10. When both sides are a golden brown, remove the pancakes using the flipper or spatula and put them on your plate. Ask an adult to turn off the stove burner.

Pour maple syrup on the pancakes and eat 'em up!

Cinnamon French Toast

French toast is a great alternative to pancakes. It's just as delicious and even easier to make. So whip up a batch for you and a pal the morning after a sleepover! This recipe serves two friends two slices of French toast each.

Ingredients You Will Need:

2 eggs
½ cup milk
¼ teaspoon cinnamon
½ teaspoon vanilla
4 slices of bread
(stale challah bread is especially good)
1 tablespoon butter
Maple syrup

Utensils You Will Need:

Measuring cups and spoons
Medium-size shallow bowl
Wire whisk
Large plate
Skillet
Pancake flipper or spatula
Range top of oven
2 plates

What You Do:

1. Crack the two eggs into the shallow bowl. To do this, gently tap an egg against the edge of one of the bowls so it cracks but doesn't mash open. Then open the two halves of the eggshell over the bowl and let the raw egg drop into the bowl. Repeat with the second egg.

2. Add the milk, cinnamon, and vanilla to the bowl, too. With the whisk, mix these ingredients together well.

3. Using clean hands, dip the slices of bread, one by one, into the mixture. Make sure to cover both sides of each slice with the batter until the slices are soaked with batter.

4. Put each batter-soaked bread slice onto a large plate.

5. 👨‍🍳 Place the skillet on one of the range top burners on the stove. Turn on the burner to medium heat.

6. Add about a third of the butter to the skillet and let it melt. Then gently pick up a slice of battered bread and put it on the skillet. Add a second slice if it fits.

7. Cook each bread slice for three to four minutes on each side. Use the pancake flipper or spatula to carefully lift up one corner of the slice — if it is golden brown underneath, it is done on that side.

8. Using the flipper or spatula, carefully flip each bread slice over and cook the other side for three to four minutes, until golden brown.

9. Use the flipper or spatula to remove the French toast and put it on the large plate.

10. Repeat with the remaining pieces of bread. Add another third of the butter to the skillet first before you put new slices of bread in to cook.

When all four slices of bread have been cooked, ask an adult to turn off the burner. Put two slices of French toast on each plate. Pour on some maple syrup and they're ready to eat. Yum!

After-school Snacks

You know how it goes — by the time you and your bud get home after a long day at school you are absolutely starving! You need a snack to hold you over until dinnertime. Instead of reaching for some junk food to fill you up, why not make one of these snacks instead!

Very Veggies and Dynamite Dips

Veggies and dip are a great after-school snack. Cutting up the veggies is the part that you can ask an adult to do. The fun part is making the delicious dips to go along with the veggie pieces. So invite some friends over and have a grown-up cut up some carrots, celery, red pepper, cucumber, or whatever. Then whip up these dips and start dunking those veggies! The dip recipes serve four to six friends.

Vege-licious Dip

Ingredients You Will Need:

One 10-ounce box frozen chopped spinach

1 cup sour cream

1 cup plain yogurt

1 envelope Knorr vegetable soup mix

Utensils You Will Need:

Measuring cup

Medium-size bowl

Wooden spoon

Colander

What You Do:

1. Before you start, take the frozen box of spinach out of the freezer and let it thaw for about an hour.

2. Put the sour cream, yogurt, and vegetable soup mix in the bowl. Stir with the wooden spoon until they are mixed together well.

3. When the spinach has thawed (this means it's no longer hard like a block), open the package and squeeze out all the water. A good way to do this is to put the spinach in a colander over the sink and gently shake the colander so the water falls through the holes and into the sink.

Put the spinach into the bowl with the sour-cream-yogurt-veggie-soup mixture and stir it until the ingredients are well blended.

Refrigerate the dip until you are ready to use it. This dip also tastes great with crackers or potato chips!

Tex-Mex Dip

Ingredients You Will Need:
One 12-ounce jar bean dip
1 cup plain yogurt
½ cup grated cheese
(Monterey Jack or cheddar)

Utensils You Will Need:
Measuring cups
Medium-size bowl
Wooden spoon

What You Do:
1. Put all the ingredients into the bowl.
2. Stir with the wooden spoon until mixed well.

Chill the dip in the fridge until you are ready to serve. (Or, if you prefer, heat the dip in the microwave to melt the cheese.) This dip also tastes great with tortilla chips!

Ooey-Gooey Cheesy Toast

On some cool days, you just need a hot snack to warm you up. Here's a tasty snack that you can easily make using a toaster oven. (Ask an adult to help if you don't feel comfortable using it yourself!) This recipe makes enough for you and a friend.

Ingredients You Will Need:

1 teaspoon dried oregano

2 slices wheat bread

½ cup (8 ounces) shredded American or cheddar cheese

Utensils You Will Need:

Measuring spoons

Toaster oven

What You Do:

1. Sprinkle ½ teaspoon of oregano onto one slice of bread, and half on the other slice.

2. Sprinkle half the shredded cheese on one slice of bread, and half on the other slice.

3. Carefully put both slices of bread onto the toaster oven tray. Toast for about one minute, or until the cheese starts to melt.

Carefully take the toasted bread out of the toaster oven. Make sure you don't touch the cheese, as it will probably be very hot. Let cool for a minute or two before eating!

Wacky Cheese Shapes 👨‍🍳

Almost everyone likes cheese—but on its own it might seem like a boring snack. Well, this recipe is anything but dull! These cheese shapes are a great snack in many ways: They are yummy, easy to make, nutritious, and really fun to eat! All you need to make these cheese shapes are cheese, candy molds, some friends, and a microwave oven! So the next time you have a couple of friends over, have fun making these silly snacks! This recipe serves four pals.

Ingredients You Will Need:

½ cup (8 ounces) shredded cheddar cheese

Utensils You Will Need:

Microwave-proof measuring cup

Microwave oven

Candy molds (These are small trays with little shaped wells in them. They are kind of like ice-cube trays except the wells are different shapes and not as deep.)

Refrigerator

What You Do:

1. 👨‍🍳 Put the cheese in the microwave-proof measuring cup and place in the microwave oven.

2. 👨‍🍳 Microwave on medium power for about two minutes, or until the cheese is melted.

3. 👨‍🍳 Carefully pour the melted cheese into the candy molds.

4. Put the cheese-filled candy molds into the refrigerator for about 20 minutes. This hardens them.

5. Remove the cheese shapes from the molds by turning the mold over and twisting and shaking it (like you do to get ice cubes out of the tray).

You can buy candy molds in whatever shapes you like (you can use molds with holiday shapes if you want to make festive cheese snacks). Then you and your friends can have fun eating the different-shaped cheese snacks. You can eat the cheese by itself or put the shapes on crackers and munch away!

Tortilla Crunchies 👨‍🍳

These chips—made from soft tortillas—taste great and are much crunchier (and healthier) than regular old tortilla or potato chips! They are yummy served with salsa or melted cheese. This recipe serves about six friends.

Ingredients You Will Need:
Twelve 6-inch soft tortillas
Vegetable-oil spray
½ teaspoon salt

Utensils You Will Need:
Cutting board
Pizza cutter or knife
Cookie sheet
Oven mitts
Oven
Large bowl

What You Do:

1. 👨‍🍳 Preheat the oven to 400°F.

2. Working with six of the tortillas, put each of the tortillas onto the cutting board and spray each with the vegetable-oil spray. Sprinkle a tiny bit of salt over each tortilla.

3. Turn each tortilla over and lightly spray and salt the other side as well.

4. After spraying and salting each one, put the six tortillas in a single stack.

5. 👨‍🍳 With an adult's help, use the pizza cutter or the knife to cut the stack of tortillas in half. Then cut the halves in half again so you have four sections.

6. 👨‍🍳 Spread one layer of tortilla pieces onto the cookie sheet. Carefully put the cookie sheet into the preheated oven.

7. 👨‍🍳 Bake the chips for eight to nine minutes, or until they are light brown at the edges and crispy. Put on the oven mitts and carefully take the cookie sheet out of the oven and pour the chips into a big bowl.

8. Repeat steps 2 through 7 with the other six tortillas.

9. 👨‍🍳 Have an adult turn off the oven when you are done.

Serve with salsa or melted cheese for you and your friends!

Quick Lunch and Dinner Dishes

Here are some recipes for when you want more than just a snack. All of these dishes can be eaten for lunch or dinner. If you have a couple of friends over, whip up one of these delicious dishes!

Turkey Wraps

Turkey wraps are quick and easy to make. You and a friend can make these all on your own. This recipe serves you and a pal—so invite a friend over for lunch!

Ingredients You Will Need:

Two 10-inch flour tortillas (tomato-flavored tortillas taste great!)

Your favorite sandwich spread (mustard, mayo,

Utensils You Will Need:

2 plates
Butter knife

guacamole, or even salsa mixed with a little sour cream are good choices)

10 ounces roasted, sliced turkey cold cuts

1 ¼ cups (10 ounces) shredded American, cheddar, or Monterey Jack cheese

What You Do:

1. Lay one tortilla on each plate.

2. Using the butter knife, spread a thin layer of your favorite sandwich spread on your tortilla. Leave about an inch around the edge of the tortilla spread-free. Have your friend do the same with her tortilla.

3. Lay half the turkey cold cuts on one of the tortillas, and half on the other one.

4. Sprinkle half the grated cheese on one of the tortillas, and half on the other one.

5. Roll up your tortilla. Have your friend do the same with hers.

Eat up!

Sandwich-in-a-Pocket

Here's an easy lunch idea that is also fun to make! These sandwiches are great when you have a few friends over because you don't need an adult's help. You and your friends can all get the ingredients ready, and then each of you can make your own sandwich just the way you like it! This recipe serves four friends.

Ingredients You Will Need:

2 large pita bread pockets

One 3-ounce package thinly sliced ham cold cuts

One 3-ounce package thinly sliced turkey cold cuts

Four ¾-ounce individually wrapped slices American cheese

4 lettuce leaves

Mayonnaise or mustard

Utensils You Will Need:

Table knife (not a sharp knife)

Large bowl

Paper towels

4 plates

What You Do:

1. Using the table knife, cut both the pita pockets in half so you have four pieces. Carefully open the bread pockets.

2. Open the packages of ham and turkey cold cuts. Using your hands, tear the slices into small pieces and put them in the bowl.

3. Open the individually wrapped cheese slices, and tear them into pieces as well. Put the cheese into the bowl with the cold cuts.

4. Mix the fillings together in the bowl with your hands.

5. Rinse the lettuce leaves in cold water and then put them on a paper towel. Pat the leaves with another paper towel to dry them.

6. Using the table knife, each friend can spread either mayonnaise or mustard on the inside of her pita pocket, as she likes.

7. Add a lettuce leaf into the pita, if you like, and then stuff some of the cheese-and-cold-cuts mixture into the pocket as well.

That's all there is to it — four great sandwiches-in-a-pocket, ready to be eaten!

PB&J Roll-ups

Sure. Everyone knows how to make a good ole peanut butter and jelly sandwich. But here's a new and improved version of the classic PB&J—a version that's just as yummy, but way more fun to make! Each piece of bread makes one sandwich, so it's really easy for you and your friends to make as many roll-ups as you need — or can eat!

Ingredients You Will Need:

1 slice white bread per friend

1 tablespoon peanut butter per friend

1 teaspoon grape or strawberry jelly per friend

Utensils You Will Need:

Rolling pin

Measuring spoons

Butter knife

1 plate for each friend

What You Do:

1. Place a slice of bread on a clean, flat surface, like a counter or tabletop.

2. Roll it out with the rolling pin until it is flat.

3. Put the peanut butter on the flattened bread and spread

it around with the butter knife. It should be a thick layer of peanut butter.

4. Put the jelly on top of the peanut butter. Spread it around with the butter knife.

5. Starting at one edge of the flattened piece of bread, carefully roll up the bread so it's a log shape.

6. Have each of your friends do the same.

You and your friends can eat the PB&J roll-ups from one end to the other, like you would bananas. Or, you can ask an adult to cut each roll-up into five or six pieces if you want bite-size morsels.

Mini-Pizzas 👨‍🍳

These individual-size mini-pizzas are easy and fun to make. They are great to make for lunch with a friend — or, if a bud is sleeping over, these pizzas are a cool, quick dinner! This recipe serves two *amigas*.

Ingredients You Will Need:

2 English muffins

4 tablespoons tomato sauce

Four ¾-ounce individually wrapped cheese slices (any type of cheese is fine)

About ½ teaspoon dried oregano

Parmesan cheese

Optional: other toppings you like (pepperoni, sliced mushrooms, sliced onions, or sliced peppers are some possibilities)

Utensils You Will Need:

Oven or toaster oven

Fork

Cookie sheet

Tablespoon

Oven mitts

Pancake flipper or spatula

2 plates

What You Do:

1. 👨‍🍳 Preheat the oven to 350°F. If you wish, you can use a toaster oven instead of an oven here. (If you're using a toaster oven instead, you don't need to preheat. Just pop the pizzas into the toaster oven and watch them; they will probably cook in less time than required for the oven.)

2. Use a fork to split the English muffins apart so you have four pieces.

3. Toast all four pieces and put them on the cookie sheet with the cut side facing up.

4. Spread one tablespoon of tomato sauce on each piece of muffin. (If you are using other toppings, put them on now, before adding the cheese.)

5. Put one slice of cheese on top of the sauce on each muffin.

6. Sprinkle two pinches of dried oregano and some Parmesan cheese on each piece. Place the muffins on the cookie sheet.

7. 👨‍🍳 Put the cookie sheet in the preheated oven. After 10 minutes, carefully open the oven door. When you see that the cheese has melted, the pizzas are done. While wearing oven mitts, take the cookie sheet out of the oven.

(If the cheese is not yet melted, close the oven and check the pizzas again two minutes later.)

8. Use the flipper or spatula to lift the pizzas off the cookie sheet and put two pizzas on each plate. Turn off the oven.

Let the pizzas cool for a couple of minutes (you don't want to burn your tongue on the hot tomato sauce!) and then enjoy this hot, yummy, good-for-you meal!

Hot Dog Roll 👨‍🍳

This is something you've probably never seen or eaten before. It's a hot dog that you eat like a hamburger on a hamburger bun. You see, the special way you prepare the hot dogs in this recipe makes them end up curling into a doughnut shape when you cook them. This is a great lunch or dinner to make when you have a few friends over. The recipe serves you and three friends — but if you have more buds to feed, it's really easy to increase the recipe. Just add an extra hot dog and hamburger roll for each additional pal.

Ingredients You Will Need:

4 hot dogs

Butter or margarine

4 hamburger rolls

Various toppings: ketchup, mustard, pickles, and relish

Utensils You Will Need:

Oven

Cutting board

Table knife

Paper towel

Cookie sheet

4 plates

Oven mitts

Pancake flipper or spatula

What You Do:

1. 🧑‍🍳 Preheat the oven to 375°F.

2. 🧑‍🍳 Put a hot dog on the cutting board. Starting about ½ inch from one end of the hot dog, use the knife to make a cut partway through the hot dog. Do not cut all the way through—you are only making little cuts in the hot dog, not slicing it into pieces.

3. Make seven more little cuts along the hot dog down to the other end. Make these same cuts on the other three hot dogs, too.

4. Rip off a little piece of paper towel and rub it onto the butter or margarine. Then rub the buttery towel across the whole cookie sheet. This is so the hot dogs don't stick to the sheet.

5. Spread the hot dogs out on the cookie sheet.

6. 🧑‍🍳 Put the cookie sheet into the preheated oven and close the oven door.

7. Let the hot dogs bake for 15 to 20 minutes. While they are cooking, pull apart the hamburger rolls and put one on each plate.

8. 👨‍🍳 After 15 to 20 minutes have passed, put on your oven mitts and open the oven door. If the hot dogs are curved around in a doughnut shape, they are done. (If they are still straight or just a little curved, let them cook for a few more minutes.)

9. 👨‍🍳 While wearing oven mitts, take the cookie sheet out of the oven and put it on the cutting board. Close the oven.

10. Use the pancake flipper or spatula to put each hot dog on a bun. Ask an adult to turn off the oven.

Serve the hot dog rolls along with the various toppings. Let your friends put on their own toppings.

Tostada Faces 👨‍🍳

Do you and your friends like Mexican food? If so, this recipe is for you! Not only does it taste good but it's also fun to make because you and your pals get to be creative and make faces with your food! This recipe serves six friends.

Ingredients You Will Need:

Two ¾-ounce individually wrapped slices of American cheese

3 fresh, washed mushrooms

6 pitted black olives

One 15-ounce can chili with beans

6 packages tostada shells

Utensils You Will Need:

Cutting board

Knife

Can opener

Spoon

Medium-size bowl

15-by-10-by-1-inch baking pan or large cookie sheet

Measuring cup

Oven

Oven mitts

Pancake flipper or spatula

6 plates

What You Do:

1. 👨‍🍳 Open the individually wrapped cheese slices and put them on the cutting board. With an adult's help, use a knife to cut each slice into three pieces that are the same size so you have six pieces total.

2. 👨‍🍳 Wash the mushrooms and put them on the cutting board. With an adult's help, cut each mushroom in half so you have six pieces total.

3. 👨‍🍳 Put the olives on the cutting board and cut each one in half (with an adult's help) so you have 12 pieces in all.

4. 👨‍🍳 Open the can of chili with a can opener. Use a spoon to empty the chili into the medium-size bowl. (The can might have sharp edges so be very careful when you are handling it.)

5. Place the tostada shells in the baking pan or on the cookie sheet. If you are using a cookie sheet you might not be able to fit all six tostadas at once. If this is the case, you can either cook them in two batches or use a second cookie sheet.

6. Using the measuring cup, put ¼ cup of chili onto each tostada shell. Spread the chili around the tostada with a spoon to about ½ inch from the edges of each shell.

7. 🍳 Preheat the oven to 350°F.

8. Now here's the really fun part! Using the cheese, mushrooms, and olives, you and your friends can make faces on your tostadas. Use a cheese slice for the mouth, a mushroom half for the nose, and two olive halves for the eyes! If you or your pals want to make a picture of something else on your tostadas, go right ahead and be creative! You can always cut up more cheese slices, mushrooms, and olives (or add some different toppings, like red and green peppers) to make whatever you want!

9. 🍳 Put the pan or cookie sheets into the preheated oven. Bake for 5 to 7 minutes, until the cheese starts to melt.

10. 🍳 Turn off the oven. Wearing oven mitts on both hands, remove the pan or cookie sheet. Use the flipper or spatula to remove the tostadas.

Put each friend's tostada creation on a separate plate and gobble up your masterpieces! You may even want to take a picture of them first!

Best Beverages, Super Shakes!

Sometimes it's just not food you're hungry for but a great shake. Here are some easy recipes for yummy beverages and shakes!

Shake-it-up Ice Cream Shake!

This thick, delicious shake is the perfect treat—part drink, part food — when you've invited a friend over to play. This recipe serves two friends.

Ingredients You Will Need:

2 cups milk

5 tablespoons chocolate syrup (or any other flavor you like)

4 tablespoons vanilla ice cream

Utensils You Will Need:

Measuring cup

Big jar with a lid (like an empty pickle jar or a pasta sauce jar)

Tablespoon

2 glasses

What You Do:

1. Pour the milk into the jar.

2. Put the chocolate syrup and the ice cream into the jar. (If you and your friend don't like chocolate, you can use a different flavor of syrup — like strawberry, coffee, or vanilla. You can also use a different flavor ice cream, too.)

3. Screw the lid on the jar very tightly.

4. Shake the jar until the ice cream has melted. You and your friend can take turns doing this.

Once the ice cream has melted, the shake is ready to drink! Unscrew the lid and pour it into the glasses. Drink and enjoy!

Fruity Fizzy Slushie 👨‍🍳

This is one of the coolest, fruitiest, and most refreshing drinks ever! It's especially great in the summer after a long day playing in the hot sun! Invite your friends over to cool down with you and this fruity fizzy slushie. The slush needs six hours to freeze, though, so prepare that part of the recipe ahead of time (like the day before). This recipe serves six friends.

Ingredients You Will Need:

One 6-ounce can frozen pineapple juice concentrate

1½ cups orange juice

1½ cups water

1 tablespoon honey

1 banana

6 cups lemon-lime soda

Utensils You Will Need:

Fork

Measuring cups and spoons

2-quart pitcher

Can opener

Wooden spoon

9-by-5-by-3-inch loaf pan

Tinfoil

Spoon

6 tall glasses

What You Do:

1. Take the can of frozen pineapple juice concentrate out of the freezer and let it soften.

2. Pour the orange juice, water, and honey into the pitcher.

3. Open the can of pineapple concentrate. (This usually comes in a plastic container. If yours is in a tin can, ask an adult to help you open the can as the edges may be sharp.) Add the concentrate to the pitcher.

4. Stir with a wooden spoon until all the ingredients are mixed together.

5. Using a fork, mash the banana and add it to the pitcher. Stir the mixture well.

6. Pour the mixture into the loaf pan and cover with foil. Put it in the freezer and let it freeze for six hours.

7. When you are ready to serve, remove the frozen mixture from the freezer. Let it soften for 20 minutes.

8. Using a spoon, scrape the surface of the frozen mixture so you get slush. Put ⅔ cup slush into each glass.

Fill the glasses the rest of the way up with lemon-lime soda, and this delicious, cool, and fizzy slushie is ready to drink! If there is any slush left over in the pan, put it back into the freezer and save it for the next time you want a fruity fizzy slushie!

Sparkling Cranberry Punch

A little sweet, a little tart, and a LOT fizzy, this is a totally refreshing drink. It's perfect on hot, hazy days when you feel like you are about to wilt. So make a batch of this punch the next time you and a group of your friends are all heated up after playing outside. You'll be ready to go again in no time. This recipe makes a large pitcherful of punch, so you and your pals can come back for seconds (and even thirds!).

Ingredients You Will Need:

1 quart chilled cranberry juice cocktail

One 5-ounce can frozen regular (or pink) lemonade concentrate

1 quart ginger ale

Sherbet (a few scoops of your favorite flavor)

Utensils You Will Need:

2-quart pitcher

Wooden spoon

1 tall glass per friend

What You Do:

1. Empty the cranberry juice and the frozen lemonade concentrate into the large pitcher. (If the lemonade concentrate is in a tin can, ask an adult to help you open the can as the edges may be sharp.)

2. Stir with wooden spoon until the concentrate is well mixed.

3. Pour in the ginger ale, and stir a few times.

4. Add the sherbet.

Drink up right away while the punch is still super-fizzy.

Strawberry-Banana Smoothie 👨‍🍳

This fruity smoothie is great to make and enjoy anytime — in the morning as part of your breakfast, with lunch, as an after-school snack, or even as a late-night treat. It's simple to make, but you do need a blender (and a grown-up to help)! This recipe makes two large smoothies so you and a friend can whip them up together!

Ingredients You Will Need:

2 cups milk

1 cup fresh and washed or frozen whole strawberries

1 banana

½ cup yogurt

1 teaspoon vanilla extract

3 teaspoons sugar

4 ice cubes

Utensils You Will Need:

Measuring cups and spoons

Blender

2 tall glasses

What You Do:

1. Put all the ingredients into the blender. Break the banana into four or five pieces first, then put the pieces in the blender.

2. 👨‍🍳 Cover the blender. Blend at high speed for 30 seconds or until it's smooth.

Pour the smoothie into two tall glasses and drink! For an extra-special touch, stick a strawberry onto the rim of each glass.

The Sweet Stuff

Dessert—the reward you get for eating all your vegetables! Now you can make your own sweet snacks. The recipes below are easy to make and so delicious! Just remember not to eat too much of the sweet stuff!

Frozen Pudding Sandwiches

These delicious treats are like ice cream sandwiches, except they contain pudding instead of ice cream. But they are just as good! Best of all, you can make them yourself! These yummy frozen "pudding-wiches" need to freeze overnight. You can make them with your friends during a sleepover party and then eat them the next day! This recipe makes 12 pudding sandwiches.

Ingredients You Will Need:

1 box instant pudding (whatever flavor you like)

2 cups cold milk

24 graham cracker squares (you can use regular, honey, cinnamon, or chocolate flavor)

Utensils You Will Need:

Medium-size bowl

Measuring cup

Wire whisk

Tablespoon

Plastic wrap

Freezer

What You Do:

1. Put the pudding mix into the bowl. Add the milk and whisk together with the wire whisk. Whisk until the mixture thickens and gets creamy.

2. Open the package of graham crackers. They come in large rectangular pieces. Break 12 of the large crackers in half along the premade lines so you have 24 squares total. (Each square will have another premade line on it so you could break it into two smaller rectangles, but don't break it in half again—leave it as a square.)

3. Using the tablespoon, spread two tablespoons of pudding each onto 12 of the graham cracker squares. Put one of the remaining squares on top of each of these to form the pudding sandwiches.

4. Wrap each pudding-filled graham cracker sandwich in plastic wrap and place them in the freezer.

Let the pudding sandwiches freeze overnight at least (if they stay in the freezer longer it's fine). When you are ready to serve them, take them out, unwrap, and eat! It's fun to try different combinations, like vanilla pudding with chocolate graham crackers or chocolate pudding with cinnamon graham crackers, or butterscotch pudding with honey graham crackers.

Crunchy Cereal Balls

These cereal balls are fun and easy, and this recipe makes enough for about four friends.

Ingredients You Will Need:

1 cup frosted flakes cereal (any kind that you like)

½ cup peanut butter

Utensils You Will Need:

Measuring cups

Medium-size bowl

Wooden spoon

Waxed paper

Freezer

What You Do:

1. Pour the frosted flakes into the bowl.

2. Slowly add the peanut butter and stir gently with the wooden spoon.

3. Continue combining the cereal and peanut butter until the cereal is completely coated with peanut butter. You can use your hands for this step if you like.

4. Using your hands, make small balls out of the mixture and put them on the waxed paper. Put the cereal balls in the freezer to harden for about 10 minutes before eating. Then enjoy these crunchy, nutty treats!

Chocolate Nutty Chews 👨‍🍳

There are times when you just have to have something chocolate and nothing else will do! These chewy, nutty, delicious cookies are super-easy to make, so go ahead and make some the next time you and your friends want a sweet, chocolate treat to eat! This recipe makes about 30 cookies.

Ingredients You Will Need:

½ cup sweetened condensed milk

3 tablespoons cocoa

1 cup chopped walnuts (or any kind of nuts you like)

Utensils You Will Need:

Oven

Can opener

Measuring cups and spoons

Medium-size bowl

Wooden spoon

Cookie sheet

Oven mitts

Pancake flipper or spatula

What You Do:

1. 👨‍🍳 Preheat the oven to 325°F.

2. 👨‍🍳 Open the can of sweetened condensed milk and pour into the bowl.

3. Add the cocoa to the bowl. Using the wooden spoon, mix the milk and cocoa together.

4. Add the chopped nuts to the bowl and stir into the milk-and-cocoa mixture.

5. Using a teaspoon, scoop up enough batter so half the spoon is covered. Drop the batter onto the cookie sheet.

6. Repeat, continuing to drop half-teaspoonfuls of batter onto the cookie sheet until the batter is gone. (The blobs of batter should be about two inches apart from one another on the cookie sheet.)

7. 👨‍🍳 Put the cookie sheet into the preheated oven.

8. 👨‍🍳 Bake for 10 to 12 minutes, then carefully remove the cookie sheet from the oven while wearing oven mitts.

9. 👨‍🍳 Turn off the oven. Let the chews cool for 10 minutes before removing them with a spatula.

Enjoy these chewy, nutty chocolate treats!

Crispy Rice Cereal Squares 👨‍🍳

Here is a recipe for delicious treats! These crisy rice cereal squares are great, there's no doubt about that, but they are also really easy to make. And crispy rice cereal squares are also really fun to make because they are great to decorate—you can add extra ingredients to them to make them really special! This recipe makes about 20 treats.

Ingredients You Will Need:

¼ cup butter or margarine (plus some to grease the pan)

4 cups miniature marshmallows

½ teaspoon vanilla extract

5 cups crispy rice cereal

Optional: Mini-chocolate chips, peanut-butter chips, mini-M&Ms, or food coloring

Utensils You Will Need:

13-by-9-inch baking pan

Paper towel

Measuring cups and spoons

Large saucepan

Range top of oven

Wooden spoon

Large bowl

What You Do:

1. Grease the baking pan. To do this, take a small piece of paper towel and scoop a little butter or margarine onto it. Spread the margarine around the bottom of the baking pan in a very thin layer.

2. 👨‍🍳 Put the butter or margarine and marshmallows in the saucepan, then add the vanilla extract. Turn on the burner on the range top to medium heat.

3. 👨‍🍳 Stir the butter or margarine, marshmallows, and vanilla with the wooden spoon until the marshmallows are melted and the mixture is thick and goopy. Turn off the burner.

4. Put the cereal into a large bowl and then pour the marshmallow mixture over it. Stir the mixture around gently so the cereal is coated.

5. Scoop the mixture into the baking pan and press down to the corners using your fingers.

Optional: You can add food coloring to the marshmallow mixture (before pouring it over the cereal) for a great holiday touch. Make a batch with some red food coloring for Valentine's Day or a batch with green food coloring for St. Patrick's Day! You can also add mini-chocolate chips, mini-M&Ms, or peanut-butter chips to the mixture just before scooping it into the baking pan to make chocolate- or peanut-butter-flavored treats!

Let the mixture cool completely, cut into squares, and serve.

Party Planning

This section will give you some great ideas for your next party, whether it's a birthday celebration with 15 people, an end-of-the-school-year get-together with seven or eight of your school pals, or a slumber party with your four best buds. Have fun!

Make-Your-Own Pizza

Just about everyone loves pizza! But the next time you are having a party, instead of getting some pies delivered, why not make your very own pizzas? Making pizzas is much easier than you might think, it's tons of fun to do, and you can have whatever weird combinations of toppings you'd like! This recipe makes two large pizzas and will serve around eight or nine friends. You can split your guests into two groups and each group can make their own pizza! The steps below are for one pizza so each group should follow them as they make their own pie.

Ingredients You Will Need:

2 packages of pizza dough (Many take-out pizza places will sell fresh pre-made pizza dough if you just ask. Or you can buy frozen dough at the supermarket.)

Flour

Vegetable-oil spray

One 16-ounce jar pizza sauce

2 tablespoons dried oregano

1 8-ounce package shredded mozzarella cheese

Extra toppings like mushrooms, spinach, goat cheese, pepperoni, sausage, or tomatoes

Utensils You Will Need:

Oven

2 round 14-inch pizza pans or 9-by-13-inch cookie sheets

Tablespoon

Dinner knife

Measuring spoons

Oven mitts

8 or 9 plates

What You Do:

1. 👨‍🍳 Preheat the oven to 400°F.

2. If the dough you bought is frozen, let it thaw for about a half hour.

3. Sprinkle some flour on a clean, flat surface, like a kitchen counter or a tabletop, and spread it around with your hand so the flour makes a pizza-size circle.

4. Plop the ball of dough on the floury spot and pound it flat with your fists. Everyone in the group can take turns pounding the dough or using their fingers to spread it out into a big, thin pancake. If you are using a cookie sheet instead of a round pizza pan, then you will need to pound it into a rectangle shape instead of a circle.

5. Pound the pizza dough until it is no more than ⅛ of an inch thick (the edges can be a little thicker because it'll be the crust). If you are having trouble doing this by pounding and pressing the dough, you can carefully lift it up and pull on the edges of the dough.

6. Lightly spray the pizza pan or cookie sheet with the vegetable-oil spray.

7. When the dough is thin enough, gently slip your fingers under the edge of the dough. Lift up the dough and carefully put it onto the pizza pan or the cookie sheet.

8. Spoon five tablespoons of pizza sauce onto the dough.

Using the back of the spoon, spread out the sauce to about an inch from the edges. Add more sauce if it doesn't cover the whole pizza.

9. Sprinkle a tablespoon of dried oregano around the whole pizza and then sprinkle half the package of mozzarella cheese around the pizza (or less if your group wants your pizza to be less cheesy).

10. Put on any other toppings your friends want, or you can do half the pizza one way and half the other. If you decide you want to add vegetable toppings like mushrooms, you will need to wash and cut the veggies into small slices or pieces before putting them on the pizza. To add spinach, you will need to cook it first in a saucepan. If you want pepperoni, you can just place some presliced pieces on top of the cheese. Ask your grown-up to help you if you need to cook some spinach or slice the pepperoni.

11. As soon as your pizza is ready, put it in the preheated oven.

12. Let the pizza cook for about 25 minutes or until the crust looks golden brown and the cheese is all melted.

13. Wearing oven mitts, take the pizza out of the oven and turn off the oven.

14. Cut each pizza into eight pieces. The sauce and cheese will be very hot, so be careful!

Make-Your-Own Pizza Variation 👨‍🍳

So, you really like the idea of making your own pizzas but you're already set on having tacos for dinner? Well, you can have it all — just make a chocolate chip pizza for dessert or a midnight snack! Instead of adding tomato sauce and cheese, you'll be sprinkling on Reese's Pieces, mini-marshmallows, and crushed Oreo cookies! This recipe serves 6–8 friends.

Ingredients You Will Need:

One package store-bought sugar cookie dough

Marshmallow Fluff

Chocolate or peanut-butter chips

Peanut butter (chunky or smooth)

Oreo cookie chunks

Reese's Pieces

Rainbow sprinkles

Mini-marshmallows

Sliced bananas or other fruit

Honey

What You Do:

1. 👨‍🍳 Preheat the oven according to the directions on the cookie dough package.

2. Open the package and round the dough into a pizza shape on the cookie sheet.

3. Bake the dough for the time noted in the directions on the package, or until light golden.

4. 👨‍🍳 Wearing oven mitts, carefully remove the cookie sheet from the oven. Allow the cookie to cool for 15–20 minutes.

5. When the cookie is cool, spread a layer of Marshmallow Fluff or peanut butter on the dough. This is your "sauce."

6. Sprinkle on the chocolate or peanut-butter chips and any other ingredients you like, such as Oreo cookie chunks, candies, sprinkles, or mini-marshmallows.

7. Add sliced bananas or other fruit.

8. Drizzle on some honey to top it all off.

9. Cut your chocolate chip pizza into wedges and serve. Yum!

Super-long Sandwich 👨‍🍳

This long sandwich is really one big loaf of bread cut up into smaller sandwiches. You and your pals can make it together. This recipe makes eight sandwiches. If you need more than that, you can just get another bread loaf and some more fillings.

Ingredients You Will Need:

1 loaf unsliced French or Italian bread (about 16 inches long)

¼ cup mayonnaise

2 teaspoons dried parsley flakes

2 teaspoons mustard

4 slices turkey cold cuts

Eight ¾-ounce slices American, cheddar, or Swiss cheese

4 slices ham cold cuts

Utensils You Will Need:

Cutting board

Bread knife

Measuring cups and spoons

Small bowl

Spoon

Butter knife

Serving platter

What You Do:

1. 👨‍🍳 Put the loaf of bread on the cutting board. Have a grown-up cut the loaf horizontally into two separate pieces.

2. Put the mayonnaise, parsley flakes, and mustard into the small bowl. Mix these ingredients together with a spoon.

3. Using the butter knife, spread the mayo-parsley-mustard mixture onto the inside of each piece of bread.

4. Add the turkey, the ham, and the cheese to one of the halves of bread; cover with the other half to make the sandwich.

5. 👨‍🍳 To serve the super-long sandwich, put it onto a large serving platter. Ask an adult to cut the sandwich into eight sections. Put the platter on a table and your friends can help themselves!

Ice Cream Sundae Bar

Mmmmm . . . ice cream sundaes—they are yummy no matter what! But they are even better when you can make them yourself. Because when you buy one in an ice cream shop, they might not have your favorite topping or they might come with too much fudge (or not enough!). Well, the next time you have a bunch of friends over, put out a sundae bar so everyone can make her own sundae exactly the way she likes! The recipe below will probably be enough for 10 to 15 people to make sundaes. If you have more guests than that, just put out more ice cream and toppings.

Ingredients You Will Need:

1 half gallon vanilla ice cream

1 half gallon chocolate ice cream

1 half gallon another flavor ice cream (strawberry or cookies 'n' cream are some other popular flavors)

One 16-ounce squeeze-bottle chocolate syrup

1 jar caramel sauce

Whatever toppings you like: for example, chocolate or rainbow sprinkles, mini-M&M's, chopped peanuts, crushed Oreo cookies, granola, sliced bananas, frozen strawberries (thawed), mini-marshmallows

Whipped cream

Utensils You Will Need:

3 ice cream scoops or large spoons

Small bowls (one per topping)

Spoons (one per topping)

A bowl and spoon for each guest

Here's the step-by-step for making a sundae bar:

At one end of a long table, put the empty bowls that the guests will make their sundaes in. Take the ice cream out of the freezer and open the containers; place them next to the bowls. Put the squeeze-bottle of chocolate syrup and the jar of caramel sauce next to the ice cream. Place the toppings in separate bowls (not the ones your guests will use!) and arrange on the table next to the chocolate syrup and caramel sauce. Add the whipped cream next to the toppings. At the very end of the table, put enough clean spoons for your guests.

Once you've got all of your ingredients on the table, put a scoop or large spoon in each of the ice cream containers, and put smaller spoons in each of the topping bowls.

That's it—your sundae bar is ready to go!

S'mores

If you've ever been camping, maybe you've already made s'mores over a campfire. Well, did you know that you can also make these delicious treats at home? They are perfect during a slumber party because they will get you and your friends in the mood for telling ghost stories in the dark! Each of your buds can put her own s'mores together. This recipe makes 12 s'mores.

Ingredients You Will Need:

24 graham cracker squares

6 Hershey's chocolate bars

12 large marshmallows

Utensils You Will Need:

Oven

Cookie sheet

Oven mitts

Spatula

12 plates

What You Do:

1. 🎩 Preheat the oven to 400°F.

2. Open the package of graham crackers. They come in large rectangular pieces. Break 12 of the large crackers in half along the premade lines so you have 24 squares total. (Each square will have another premade line on it but don't break it in half again—leave it as a square.)

3. Open the chocolate bars and break each one in half so you have 12 large pieces.

4. Open the bag of marshmallows.

5. Each guest should take two graham cracker squares, one piece of chocolate, and one large marshmallow.

6. Each guest can then build her own s'more this way: Put a graham cracker square down on the table. Put the piece of chocolate on top of the graham cracker. Put the marshmallow on top of the chocolate. Cover with the other graham cracker square.

7. Each guest should then put her s'more on the cookie sheet (and remember which one is hers).

8. 🎩 After everyone has made her s'more, put the cookie sheet into the oven. Let the s'mores cook for three minutes.

9. 👨‍🍳 Wearing oven mitts, take the cookie sheet out of the oven. Turn off the oven.

10. With a spatula, put each person's s'more on a plate.

Wait a couple of minutes for the s'mores to cool. Then each person should pick hers up, press down on both graham crackers so the melted marshmallow spreads out, and then eat!

Peanut-Butter Putty

Here is another get-your-hands-messy concoction. Except this one isn't exactly a dessert — although you CAN eat it, and it tastes pretty good. But the best part of this recipe isn't how it tastes. Have you ever been told, "Don't play with your food"? Well, you won't hear that here! This peanut-butter putty is MEANT to be played with—and then eaten afterward (if you want). So go ahead and play with your food. This recipe makes enough putty for you and a friend to play with.

Ingredients You Will Need:

1 cup peanut butter
1 cup powdered milk
1 tablespoon honey

Utensils You Will Need:

Measuring cups and spoons
Medium-size bowl
Wooden spoon
Waxed paper

What You Do:

1. Put the peanut butter into the bowl.

2. Add the powdered milk. Stir with the wooden spoon for about five minutes until the ingredients are mixed together well.

3. Add the honey. Stir again until the honey is mixed in and the putty is no longer sticky. If you need to, finish combining the ingredients with your hands.

That's it! Your peanut-butter putty is ready for you to sculpt and mold however you and your friend like. (Create your works of art on waxed paper to protect the counter or table from getting all sticky.) Then afterward, go ahead and eat your creations!

Holiday Food Ideas

Holidays are so much fun—and they are even more exciting if you decide to celebrate with your friends! But you might not have any ideas about what you could serve. Here are a few recipes that are sure to be hits!

Jiggly Hearts for Valentine's Day

Have a Valentine's Day party and serve these yummy, fun-to-eat, easy-to-make jiggly hearts. It's a sweet treat for the sweetest holiday. Serve these hearts on a red or pink plate for an extra Valentine's touch. This recipe makes 8 to 10 servings.

Ingredients You Will Need:

2½ cups water

2 packages cherry, strawberry, or raspberry gelatin mix

1 package instant vanilla pudding mix

1 cup cold milk

Vegetable-oil spray

Utensils You Will Need:

Measuring cups

Electric teakettle or small saucepan

2 medium-size bowls

Wooden spoon

Wire whisk

13-by-9-by-2-inch dish or pan

Heart-shaped cookie cutter

What You Do:

1. Boil the water in an electric teakettle or in a saucepan. If you use a saucepan, you will need an adult's help turning the burner on and off.

2. Put the two packages of gelatin into one of the medium-size bowls. When the water is boiling, pour it into the bowl. Stir with the wooden spoon until all the gelatin powder is dissolved. Set this mixture aside for a half hour to cool.

3. Put the vanilla pudding mix into the other medium-size

bowl. Add the milk and whisk together until the mixture thickens and gets creamy and pudding-like.

4. Scoop the pudding into the liquid gelatin with the wooden spoon. Whisk until the gelatin and pudding are mixed together well.

5. Spray a thin coating of vegetable-oil spray on the 13-by-9-by-2-inch dish.

6. Pour the gelatin-and-pudding mixture into the dish.

7. Refrigerate until it's firm, about an hour. Then use the heart-shaped cookie cutter to cut out jiggly Valentine's Day heart treats!

Homemade Limeade for St. Patrick's Day

Here is a refreshing drink that you can make for your friends on St. Patrick's Day. It's sort of like lemonade, only it's green! This recipe serves eight pals.

Ingredients You Will Need:

1 cup sugar

12 limes

6 cups cold water

Green food coloring (optional)

Utensils You Will Need:

Measuring cup

Pitcher

Wooden spoon

Knife

8 glasses

Juicer

What You Do:

1. Put the sugar into the pitcher.

2. Cut each lime in half so you have 24 halves. Use a juicer to squeeze the juice out of each lime half into the pitcher.

3. Add the cold water to the pitcher and stir with the wooden spoon.

4. If you'd like, add two drops of food coloring to make the limeade a brighter green color. Stir.

Pour into the glasses and add ice cubes. For an extra touch, make green ice cubes with water and food coloring and add them to the limeade for an even greener drink!

Halloween Sewer Soda

This soda looks like dirty, gross sewer water — but it tastes really good! For an extra Halloween effect, buy an ice-cube tray with Halloween shapes and add creepy ice cubes to the sewer soda! You can also float a couple of black plastic spiders in the pitcher to really gross out your guests! This recipe serves 10 to 12 friends.

Ingredients You Will Need:

1 envelope unsweetened grape flavor Kool-Aid mix

1 envelope unsweetened orange flavor Kool-Aid mix

2 cups sugar

12 cups cold water

1 quart bottle chilled ginger ale

Utensils You Will Need:

Large pitcher

Measuring cup

Wooden spoon

What You Do:

1. Open both envelopes of Kool-Aid mix and pour them into the pitcher.

2. Add the sugar to the pitcher, too.

3. Add the water to the pitcher and mix together with the wooden spoon until all the powder has dissolved.

4. Just before you are ready to serve, add the ginger ale.

Halloween Dirt Cups

Your guests will love these treats, which look like cups of dirt with creepy-crawlies climbing out of them but which taste sweet and cool! This recipe serves 10 friends.

Ingredients You Will Need:

3½ cups Cool Whip topping

1 package instant chocolate pudding

1 cup cold milk

1 package chocolate sandwich cookies

Decorations: gummy worms, gummy frogs, gummy bugs, and chopped peanuts

Utensils You Will Need:

Measuring cup

Medium-size bowl

Wire whisk

Large spoon

Large resealable plastic bag

Rolling pin

Ten 7-ounce plastic cups

What You Do:

1. Take the Cool Whip out of the freezer and let it thaw for 15 minutes.

2. Put the pudding mix into the bowl. Add the milk and whisk together with the wire whisk until the mixture thickens and gets creamy and pudding-like.

3. Gently and slowly stir in the whipped topping with the spoon.

4. Put the chocolate sandwich cookies into the resealable plastic bag and seal the bag. Roll the rolling pin over the bag. Press down with the rolling pin until the cookies are all crushed. When you are finished, they should look like dirt.

5. Spoon some chocolate pudding into each cup. There should be around a ½ inch of pudding in the bottom of each cup.

6. Spoon a ¼ inch of crushed cookie into each cup.

7. Repeat steps 6 and 7 until the cup is full and then top with crushed cookie.

8. Refrigerate the dirt cups for a couple of hours. Right before you are ready to serve, you can decorate them. Stick gummy worms into the dirt cups so it looks like

they are crawling out, or place gummy frogs or gummy bugs on top of the "dirt." Sprinkle chopped peanuts on top, which look like pebbles.

If you find any other candies that look like bones, gravestones, or anything else that's creepy, decorate the dirt cups with those, too!

Rudolph's Antlers for Christmas

Here is a great treat to make that's a little different from most of the holiday recipes you'll find out there. Your guests will get a real kick out of these "antlers." This recipe makes 24 sweet treats.

Ingredients You Will Need:

1 cup semisweet chocolate chips

1 cup butterscotch chips

One 3-ounce can chow mein noodles

12 maraschino cherries

Utensils You Will Need:

Medium-size saucepan

Range top of oven

Measuring cup

Wooden spoon

Waxed paper

Cookie sheet

Tablespoon

2 teaspoons

Knife

What You Do:

1. 👨‍🍳 Put the saucepan on the range top of the oven. Put the chocolate and butterscotch chips into the saucepan.

2. 👨‍🍳 Turn the burner to medium heat. Melt the chips, stirring often with the wooden spoon.

3. 👨‍🍳 Turn off the burner and remove the pan from the hot burner.

4. Put the chow mein noodles into the saucepan and stir them so they get covered with the melted chip mixture.

5. Put waxed paper onto the cookie sheet.

6. Spoon a tablespoon of the mixture onto the waxed-paper-covered cookie sheet. Using the two teaspoons, shape the mixture into a V shape so it looks like antlers. Each set of "antlers" should be about 2 inches across.

7. 👨‍🍳 Cut the cherries in half. Press a cherry half into each cookie where the two "antlers" meet at the bottom.

Chill the cookies in the refrigerator for one to two hours before serving.

Keep on Cookin'!

Now that you've (hopefully!) tried some of the dishes in this book, don't stop cooking! There are tons of cookbooks out there that are geared specifically to kids. In addition, there are lots of Web sites out there with great kids' recipes! Here are a few you should definitely check out:

- The Kid Kitchen Web site at *http://members.tripod.com/~AngieCooks/kids/Recipes.html* has lots of easy snack, drink, lunch, and dessert recipes. This site tells you which recipes require stove-top or oven cooking. You can look up recipes by their specific names or by categories. The site also has a Halloween recipe section.

- The Kids Recipes from SOAR (Searchable Online Archive of Recipes) Web site at *http://soar.berkeley.edu/recipes/kids/index0.html* has an alphabetized list of over 150 kids' recipes. Not all the recipes are easy because some are geared to adults cooking for kids, but the huge number and variety of recipes make it worth checking out! You will find basic recipes, like popcorn balls and couscous, as well as wilder recipes for dinosaur eggs and pizza pinwheels!

- The KidsHealth.org Kids Recipes Web site at *http://kidshealth.org/kid/games/recipe/* emphasizes healthy recipes that are geared specifically to kid chefs. The recipes are divided into category by type of food (including drinks, breads, breakfasts, dinners, and fruits and veggies) and they are very easy to follow with clear steps. The site includes cooking safety rules.

- Kids Kings of the Kitchen: *www.scoreone.com/kids_kitchen/index.htm* features recipes created by kids all over the world. You can submit your favorite recipes, too.

So keep on cooking! Before you know it you'll be moving on to more and more advanced and amazing recipes! Have fun!

Recipes of My Own